MW00623334

ISRAEL

Whose Land is it Anyway?

Israel: Who's Land is it Anyway?

Copyright © 2019 by The Friends of Israel Gospel Ministry, Inc. Bellmawr, New Jersey 08099

Unless otherwise noted all Scripture quotations are taken from the New King James Version®. Copyright © 1982 by Thomas Nelson, Inc. Used by permission.

All rights reserved. Printed in the United States of America. No part of this book may be reproduced, stored in a retrieval system, or transmitted, in any form or by any means, electronic, mechanical, photocopying, recording, otherwise, without prior written permission of the publisher.

For information, address The Friends of Israel Gospel Ministry, Inc., P.O. Box 908, Bellmawr, NJ 08099.

Library of Congress Catalog Card Number: 2019952752

ISBN-13 978-1-930518-01-8

Cover by Catie Almacellas.

Visit our website at foi.org

Acknowledgements
Our deepest thanks to Jennifer Miles, a Christian apologist who devoted countless months researching and writing this booklet while working as an editor for The Friends of Israel Gospel Ministry.

INTRODUCTION

Israel. A word that instantly evokes emotion in countless people the world over. For some, the mention of Israel awakens strong feelings of anger and hatred. For others, it arouses sentiments of love and passionate support. Few remain simply indifferent.

Every day media stories flood our inboxes, televisions, and news feeds, informing us of more attacks in the Middle East. More innocent lives lost. More confusion over who is the perpetrator and who is the victim.

Some remember the horrific story of the Fogel family massacre. On a seemingly ordinary Friday night in 2011, 12-year-old Tamar Fogel returned home to find her mom, dad, and three of her five young siblings brutally stabbed to death and shot.

A police investigation revealed that the perpetrators were two Arab teenagers from the nearby village of Awarta. Cousins Amjad and Hakim Awad proudly told investigators they waited for a Friday night to carry out the attack since they knew Jewish families would be home celebrating Shabbat, the Jewish Sabbath.

The two young Arabs jumped the security fence surrounding Itamar—a Jewish community in Judea and Samaria—and crawled through the window of the Fogels' home. Armed with machetes, wire-cutting pliers, and a stolen M-16 rifle, Amjad and Hakim stabbed parents Ruth and Ehud, 11-year-old Yoav; 4-year-old Elad; and 3-month-old Hadas. The attack left Tamar and her two remaining siblings orphaned.

Such brutal attacks on innocent civilians commonly occur in Israel. Arab-Palestinians claim their violent actions are justified because of Israel's occupation, theft of Palestinian land, and refusal to grant Palestinian refugees a "right of return" and/or reparations.

Israel claims Arab-Palestinians are responsible for perpetuating the Arab-Israeli conflict because of their deep-seated anti-Semitism, desire to destroy Israel, refusal to seek peace and recognize Israel's statehood, and commitment to terrorism. Israel argues it must use force to defend itself because it is surrounded by enemies determined to annihilate the Jewish state.

Both Jews and Arabs claim divine, legal, and historical rights to the land. But both cannot be right. This booklet examines both the Jewish and Arab claims and argues that the land belongs to Israel biblically, historically, and legally. The section describing Israel's biblical right to the land also takes a look at Supersessionism, often called Replacement Theology, and shows why Christians should support Israel.

We will discuss the hot-button issues of Israel's "occupation" and the Arab demand for a "right of return" for Palestinian refugees. Although Israel maintains the legal and biblical rights to reside in Gaza, the West Bank (Judea and Samaria), and all of Jerusalem, it has historically displayed a willingness to give up its rights in these regions to seek peace with its Arab neighbors. In response to Israel's concessions, the Arabs increased violence and refused to negotiate with Israel.

We also will argue that the Arab demand for Israel to grant a "right of return" and reparations to 4.5 million registered Arab-Palestinian refugees is unfounded. We will show how the United Nations Relief and Works Agency (UNRWA) and Arab states exaggerate the number of actual refugees, have created and perpetuated the problem, and already have received compensation for the actual number of refugees who fled Israel during the war.

Ultimately, lasting peace will only reign in the Middle East when the Messiah returns to sit on David's throne in Jerusalem. Then and only then will the Jewish people finally live in peace in all of the land God promised them.

Jewish Claims

JEWISH CLAIM ONE:

Israel Has the Divine Deed to the Land

God gave the land of Israel to the Jewish people in an everlasting covenant. The Lord promised Abraham, "To your descendants I have given this land, from the river of Egypt to the great river, the River Euphrates. Also I give to you and your descendants after you the land in which you are a stranger, all the land of Canaan, as an everlasting possession; and I will be their God" (Gen. 15:18; 17:8).

God reiterated this promise to Abraham's son Isaac instead of Ishmael and then confirmed it to Isaac's son Jacob instead of Esau (vv. 18–21; 28:13–15). God is faithful to His promises. The psalmist wrote of the Lord:

> He remembers His covenant forever, the word which He commanded, for a thousand generations, the covenant which He made with Abraham, and His oath to Isaac, and confirmed it to Jacob for a statute, to Israel as an everlasting covenant, saying, "To you I will give the land of Canaan as the allotment of your inheritance" (Ps. 105:8–11).

God's promise to Abraham, Isaac, and Jacob was unilateral and unconditional. That means its fulfillment depends on God, not man. Bible scholar Dr. Randall Price explained, "The Abrahamic Covenant is unconditional because God initiated it and has personally assumed the obligation for its fulfillment. Restoration to the Land was therefore possible, for even sin on the part of the Jewish people cannot keep the promise of God's own covenant from being fulfilled."[1]

Although the Lord scattered the Israelites because of sin and unbelief, He promised to regather them to the Promised Land because of His faithfulness, not theirs:

> Thus says the Lord GOD: "I do not do this for your sake, O house of Israel, but for My holy name's sake, which you have profaned among the nations wherever you went. For I will take you from among the nations, gather you out of all countries, and bring you into your own

land" (Ezek. 36:22, 24).

The Lord will keep His promise to Abraham, Isaac, and Jacob for His name's sake. He has already begun to gather the Jewish people back to the land He promised them: The establishment of the modern State of Israel is proof.

God's promise to Israel will be fully realized at the Messiah's return. Jesus will physically return to the Mount of Olives in Jerusalem and destroy Israel's enemies once and for all. The prophet Zechariah wrote,

> *It shall be in that day that I [Israel's Messiah] will seek to destroy all the nations that come against Jerusalem. And I will pour on the house of David and on the inhabitants of Jerusalem the Spirit of grace and supplication; then they will look on Me whom they pierced* (Zech. 12:9–10).

In that day, the Messiah will set up His Kingdom and reign from David's throne; and the nation of Israel will finally dwell in all of the land God promised to give it (Isa. 2:2–4; Ezek. 37:24–28; Hos. 3:4–5).

While most evangelical Christians strongly support Israel and believe God gave the land to the Jewish people as an eternal possession, some deny the modern State of Israel belongs to the Jewish people because of a false theology called Supersessionism.

Supersessionism, also known as Replacement Theology, teaches that the church of Jesus Christ has superseded or replaced the Jewish people as God's covenant people. One prominent theologian in this camp, Bruce K. Waltke, wrote that the New Testament teaches the "hard fact that national Israel and its law have been permanently replaced by the church and the New Covenant."[2]

Some believe God replaced Israel with the church because of Israel's disobedience. This view is called "punitive" Supersessionism.[3] Many in the Patristic Era held this view. Origen (c. 185–254) wrote, "And we say with confidence that they [the Jews] will never be restored to their former condition. For they committed a crime of the most unhallowed kind."[4]

Other supersessionists assert the church replaced Israel merely because Israel's role was no longer needed in God's plan. This view is called "economic" Supersessionism.[5]

Richard Kendall Soulen explained Supersessionism in the following way:

> *God chose the Jewish people after the fall of Adam in order to prepare the world for the coming of Jesus Christ, the Savior. After Christ came, however, the special role of the Jewish people came to an end and its place was taken by the church, the new Israel.*[6]

According to Supersessionism, God will not fulfill His promise to give Israel the land as an everlasting possession, nor will He restore Israel to a special place of service among the nations when Christ returns.[7] Supersessionists admit God chose Israel as His chosen nation and servant in the Old Testament, but they believe that role was temporary. Since Christ has come, they argue the following:

Jesus is "true" Israel."

1. Jesus thus assumes and fulfills Israel's mediatorial role.
2. All those in Christ are also "true Israel."
3. Therefore, no future role remains for ethnic Israel.[8]

Scripture does not support such an argument.

SUPERSESSIONISTS CLAIM: JESUS IS "TRUE ISRAEL."

Supersessionist theologians argue that Jesus as "true Israel" has replaced ethnic Israel because New Testament authors such as Matthew linked Israel's experiences with Jesus. For example, Matthew quoted the Hebrew prophet Hosea's account of Israel's Exodus out of Egypt as prophetic fulfillment of Christ's departure from Egypt (Mt. 2:15; cf. Hos. 11:1).

Robert B. Strimple argued, "Christ is the true Israel of God, the one in whom Israel's history is recapitulated and God's purposes for Israel come to fulfillment."[9]

But simply acknowledging the fact that New Testament authors identify Jesus with Israel does not negate the legitimacy of ethnic Israel. Nowhere does Scripture say such a thing. In fact, Christ's identification with Israel provides all the more reason to believe He will fulfill His promises to Israel. He, as Israel's corporate Head, is able to restore the nation.[10]

To claim that because Christ is "true Israel," ethnic Israel no longer exists in God's plan is akin to saying that because Christ is the "ulti-mate" Man (Rom. 5:12–21), God no longer has a plan for the rest of humanity.[11] Jesus represents Israel; He doesn't replace it.

Some supersessionists also claim that because the New Testament speaks of Jesus as fulfilling Isaiah's prophecies about the "Servant of Israel," any future prophecies concerning Israel have "vanished" in Jesus Christ. Kim Riddlebarger propounded, "The New Testament writers claimed that Jesus was the true Israel of God and the fulfillment of Old Testament prophecies. So what remains of the dispensationalists' case that these prophecies will yet be fulfilled in a future millennium? They vanish in Jesus Christ, who has fulfilled them."[12]

Isaiah 49 clearly contradicts this view.[13] The prophet Isaiah said that the Lord's Servant, Israel (Messiah Jesus in this context), would restore national Israel:

> *And He said to me, "You are My servant, O Israel, in whom I will be glorified." And now the LORD says, who formed Me from the womb to be His Servant, to bring Jacob back to Him, so that Israel is gathered to Him, . . . "It is too small a thing that You should be My Servant to raise up the tribes of Jacob, and to restore the preserved ones of Israel; I will also give You as a light to the Gentiles, that You should be My salvation to the ends of the earth"* (vv. 3, 5–6).

Isaiah calls the servant "Israel," yet clearly distinguishes the Servant from national Israel. The Lord gave the Servant a commission: "to bring Jacob back to Him," to gather Israel to the Lord, and "to restore . . . Israel." This Servant would also be a "light to the Gentiles" to bring God's "salvation to the ends of the earth." Jesus has brought salvation to the Gentiles, and He will restore Israel at His return.

Isaiah 52:13–14; 53:3–6 also distinguishes the Lord's "Servant" from national Israel:

> *Behold, My Servant shall deal prudently; . . . His visage was marred more than any man, and His form more than the sons of men. He is despised and rejected by men, a Man of sorrows and acquainted with grief. And we [Israel] hid, as it were, our faces from Him; He was despised, and we did not esteem Him. Surely He has borne our*

griefs and carried our sorrows; yet we esteemed Him stricken, smitten by God, and afflicted. But He was wounded for our transgressions, He was bruised for our iniquities; the chastisement for our peace was upon Him, and by His stripes we are healed. . . . The LORD has laid on Him the iniquity of us all.

The Lord sent the Servant—Messiah Jesus—to suffer and die for the nation's sins (as well as for the sins of the world, since God extended salvation to the Gentiles through Jesus). God gave Israel a Messiah that would be so identified with the Jewish people that He would even suffer for them.

The Jewish people have suffered persecution throughout the ages, but Jesus' torture and death shows that God is not removed from their suffering. They can rejoice that their own Messiah so identifies with them in that He also experienced tremendous suffering.

SUPERSESSIONISTS CLAIM: JESUS FULFILLS ISRAEL'S MEDIATORIAL ROLE.

Supersessionists claim that since Christ is the only Mediator between God and humanity (1 Tim. 2:5), Israel serves no purpose in Christ's future Kingdom. The context of 1 Timothy 2, however, concerns salvation. Only Christ mediates our salvation.[14]

But Scripture is replete with references to others serving as mediators in Christ's Kingdom:
- The church will reign and rule over nations (Rev. 2:26; 5:10).
- Jesus promised His 12 apostles they would judge the tribes of Israel (Mt. 19:28).
- Nations (including Israel) will reign over the new earth (Rev. 22:3–5).[15]

Just as God gave Adam and Eve ruling/mediatorial tasks on Earth before the Fall, so too will He give humanity ruling tasks in His Kingdom. Israel will have the unique role of ministering spiritually to the world and leading the Gentiles in worship (Ex. 19:5–6; Isa. 61:6; Zech. 8:23).[16]

SUPERSESSIONISTS CLAIM: THE CHURCH IS ISRAEL BECAUSE THE CHURCH IS PART OF CHRIST.

Supersessionism holds that since Christ is true Israel and Christians are joined to Christ, therefore the church is the new Israel. Vern Poythress advocates this position:

> *Because Christ is an Israelite and Christians are in union with Christ, Christians partake of the benefits promised to Israel and Judah in Jeremiah. . . . Israel and Judah themselves undergo a transformation at the first coming of Christ, because Christ is the final, supremely faithful Israelite. Around him all true Israel gathers.*[17]

Some advocate this position by appealing to Paul's calling of believing Gentiles "sons of Abraham" in Galatians 3:7. But Paul called believing Gentiles "sons of Abraham" to explain his point that Gentiles are justified by faith, according to the promise God gave Abraham: "In you all the nations shall be blessed" (v. 8).[18]

Through Abraham's seed, the Messiah came and justified Gentiles by faith. But Paul never said Gentiles are now a part of Israel. He said both believing Gentiles and believing Jews are sons of Abraham.

The New Testament refers to Israel 73 times. Seventy of those times clearly reference national Israel. Only three references that mention Israel are debated and used by supersessionists to claim Israel refers to the church: Romans 9:6; 11:25–26; and Galatians 6:16.[19]

Romans 9:6: "For they are not all Israel who are of Israel." Paul did not say Gentiles are Israel here. He merely distinguished between believing and unbelieving Israel. John Murray, commenting on the passage, said, "There is an 'Israel' within ethnic Israel."[20]

Romans 11:25–26: "Blindness in part has happened to Israel until the fullness of the Gentiles has come in. And so all Israel will be saved." How can the word *Israel* in this passage refer to the church (Jewish and Gentile believers in Christ) when it describes Israel as being blinded until all of God's called Gentiles are saved? Paul explained that much of ethnic Israel has been blinded from the truth of Jesus' identity, but in the future "all Israel will be saved" and recognize their Messiah (cf. Zech. 12:10).

Why would Israel in Romans 11:26 be different from the ethnic Israel Paul described in verse 25? The other 10 references to "Israel" in chapters 9—11 also clearly refer to national Israel. Murray explained, "It is exegetically impossible to give to 'Israel' in this verse any other

denotation than that which belongs to the term throughout this chapter.
. . . It is of ethnic Israel Paul is speaking and Israel could not possibly include Gentiles."[21]

Galatians 6:16: "And as many as walk according to this rule, peace and mercy be upon them, and upon the Israel of God." Within context, Paul had just rebuked the teaching of the Judaizers, a Jewish sect that claimed to believe in Jesus but added the works of the Mosaic Law to salvation. Paul commended the Jewish believers in Christ who refused to believe the Judaizers' distortion of the gospel by calling them the "Israel of God."[22]

In none of Paul's letters did he ever refer to Gentiles as "Israel." And in these three passages, he narrowed his usage of the term to refer specifically to Jewish believers in Christ.

SUPERSESSIONISTS CLAIM: NATIONAL ISRAEL HAS NO FUTURE ROLE IN GOD'S PLAN

Since Christ and the church have permanently replaced Israel, supersessionists claim, no role remains for national Israel in Christ's future Kingdom. But this view contradicts multiple New Testament verses that affirm Israel's place in the Millennial Kingdom.

In Matthew 19:28, Jesus told His disciples, "Assuredly I say to you, that in the regeneration, when the Son of Man sits on the throne of His glory, you who have followed Me will also sit on twelve thrones, judging the twelve tribes of Israel." Jesus noted here the significance of the "twelve tribes of Israel" in the future Kingdom. Bible scholar Michael J. Vlach explained,

> Thus, in the eschaton Jesus, the true Israel, exists alongside "the twelve tribes of Israel," which refers to the nation Israel. Jesus does not indicate that His identity as "true Israel" extinguishes national Israel's identity and significance.[23]

In Acts 1:6, Jesus' disciples asked Him, "Lord, will You at this time restore the kingdom to Israel?" The disciples already knew the gospel—that Jesus' death and resurrection purchased salvation for Jews and Gentiles alike, for all who place their faith in Him. Yet they understood the prophets foretold of a time when the Lord would "restore the kingdom to Israel."

Jesus did not rebuke or correct His disciples. He answered them, "It is not for you to know times or seasons which the Father has put in His own authority" (v. 7). He instructed them to focus on proclaiming the gospel and indirectly affirmed their understanding that God would restore national Israel in the future.[24]

In Revelation 7:4–8, Vlach said, the apostle John "pointed to future significance for the twelve tribes of Israel."[25] John described Israel's distinction during the Great Tribulation: an angel will seal 144,000 Jewish people—12,000 from each tribe of Israel. He set them apart from other "nations, tribes, peoples, and tongues" (v. 9).

So the New Testament affirms the Old Testament's teaching that God has a future plan for national Israel. God will faithfully keep His promises to His Chosen People and restore them to the land He promised them in the Abrahamic Covenant—for His name's sake.

JEWISH CLAIM TWO:
The Jewish People Have a Historical Tie to the Land

The Jewish people have a 3,500-year connection with the land of Israel. Palestinian propaganda, however, seeks to deny Israel's ancient history in the land, especially in Jerusalem. Many Palestinian Authority (PA) leaders have overtly denied the historical existence of a Jewish Temple in Jerusalem and claimed the Arab-Palestinians occupied the Temple Mount and Jerusalem centuries before the Jewish people.[26] PA President Mahmoud Abbas' former Minister of Religious Affairs Mahmoud Al-Habbash said Jerusalem has been "throughout history, the capital of the Palestinian state and the capital of the Palestinian people."[27]

Similarly, Abbas-appointed Grand Mufti of Jerusalem Muhammad Ahmad Hussein stated the following:

They [Jews] want to say or suggest that this place [i.e., the Temple Mount] was once, according to their claim, a Temple. However, in truth, there never was a Temple in any period, nor was there, at any time, any place of worship for the Jews or others at the Al-Aqsa Mosque site [i.e., which was built on the Temple Mount in AD 705].[28]

Such statements not only contradict the Bible, they contradict archaeology. Archaeological discoveries have confirmed what the Bible has claimed for years: Israel is the Jewish people's ancient homeland, and Jerusalem is its capital.

One such discovery took place in 1993, when a team of archaeologists discovered a 9th-century BC inscription at Tel Dan, a mound in northern Galilee. The artifact read, "House of David" and "King of Israel."[29]

In 2011, the Israel Antiquities Authority opened an archaeological dig site to the public where people could walk through the remains of the first Temple. One of the site's excavators believes he found the "Water Gate" mentioned in Nehemiah 3:25–26. Others found remains from the walls Solomon ordered the stone masons to build to protect the city.[30]

Such discoveries merely scratch the surface of the many archaeological findings that support the Jewish historical claim to the land of Israel—more than 16 centuries before Muhammad founded Islam and long before the Arab conquest in the land.

JEWISH CLAIM THREE:
The Jewish People Have Had a Continuous Presence in the Land

Many anti-Zionists falsely believe that after the Romans forced the Jewish people to leave the land in AD 70, no Jews remained there; then 1,800 years later, Jewish people returned and demanded their country back.[31]

But that belief is not true. Jewish people have lived in the land for the past 3,500 years, and those who were exiled maintained a strong spiritual, emotional, and cultural connection to it.[32]

Physical presence. Despite invasions and captivities, the Jewish people have maintained an uninterrupted presence in Israel since the days of Joshua. In 1406 BC, the Israelite army took possession of Canaan (Israel) under Joshua's leadership, and the Jewish people established their own national language, culture, and civilization, which have remained in the land since that time.

After the Assyrians took the northern kingdom of Israel into captivity in 722 BC and the Babylonians took the southern kingdom of Judah into captivity in 586 BC, a remnant of Jewish people still remained in the land. Likewise, when the Romans exiled large numbers of Jewish people after the First Jewish Revolt (AD 66–73), a remnant remained and revolted again in the Second Jewish Revolt (AD 132–135).

The Jewish people temporarily won national sovereignty in the land; but soon after, Rome ended Jewish rule and imposed greater restrictions. The Jewish people continued to live in the land under Roman rule (AD 135–391), Roman Byzantine Christian rule (AD 391–636), and then under Muslim rule from AD 638 until the creation of the modern State of Israel.[33]

Many historical resources refer to large communities of Jewish people in the land for the past 19 centuries. In the ninth century, Jewish communities in Jerusalem and Tiberias were reestablished; in the 11th century, Jewish communities grew in Rafah, Gaza, Ashkelon, Jaffa, and Caesarea. In the 13th and 14th centuries, many rabbis and Jewish people immigrated to Jerusalem, Safed, and Galilee.[34]

So when the first Zionist pioneers made Aliyah (immigrated) to Israel between 1882 and 1903, they found already-established Jewish communities that had existed in the land for centuries.

SPIRITUAL AND EMOTIONAL CONNECTION

Jewish people in the Diaspora, though not physically present in the land, nonetheless reserved a strong connection to it and a longing to return. Many maintained their distinct cultural and religious identities, despite being scattered among the nations.

Jewish people express this deep-seated connection to Israel in many ways. One way includes remembering the destruction of the Temple. On Tisha B'Av, Jewish people everywhere fast and mourn the destruction of the first and second Temples. They also commemorate the Temple at weddings, when the bridegroom traditionally breaks a glass during the ceremony as a reminder of the Temples' destruction.[35]

Jewish people yearn for Israel in their prayers and songs about Jerusalem. Every year at Passover, they end the seder dinner with the exclamation, "Next year in Jerusalem!"[36] Many regularly recite the words of the psalmist: "If I forget you, O Jerusalem, let my right hand forget its skill. If I do not remember you, let my tongue cling to the roof of my mouth—if I do not exalt Jerusalem above my chief joy" (Ps. 137:5–6).

Many write songs and poems to express their longing to return to Israel. Yehuda Ha-Levi (1085–1141), a famous Jewish poet in medieval Spain, wrote one such poem of lament:

> *My heart is in the East and I am at the edge of the West; Then how can I taste what I eat, how can I enjoy it? How can I fulfill my vows and pledges? While Zion is in the domain of Edom, and I am in the bonds of Arabia? It would be easy for me to leave behind all the good things of Spain; it would be glorious to see the dust of the ruined shrine.*[37]

JEWISH CLAIM FOUR:
Israel Bought and Settled the Land

Palestinian advocates often claim the Jewish people illegally displaced a large, stable, and long-term Palestinian-Arab population that existed in the land for centuries. They say the Jewish people stole masses of land from local Arab fellahin (farmers). Arab professor Mohammad Abu Laila from Al-Azhar University in Cairo stated, "The Jews stole our land. What else do you want us to do, just go away?"[38]

Such statements, however, are contrary to the historical evidence. Before the First Aliyah, the land was underpopulated and largely nonarable. When European Jewish refugees arrived, they purchased arid desert from absentee landlords and, over time, transformed it into fruitful, inhabitable land.

UNDERPOPULATED

Palestinian propagandists often claim the Jews displaced a large population of thriving Arabs. But statistics reveal the entire population of the land did not exceed half a million at the time of the First Aliyah in the early 1880s; even more, the total population of the portion of land the United Nations (UN) would later partition to Israel was only between 100,000 and 150,000 at the time.[39]

Pro-Palestinian historian Benny Morris conceded, "Only 'several thousand' families were displaced following land sales to Jews between the 1880s and the late 1930s."[40]

Alan Dershowitz, Harvard Law School professor and distinguished expert on the Middle East conflict, said of the numbers, "This is a fraction of the number of people displaced by the Egyptian construction of the Aswan Dam, the Iraqi displacement of the Marsh Arabs, and other forced movements by Arab governments of fellow Arabs."[41] And of those who were displaced, many were recent migrants from Turkey, Greece, Algeria, and Egypt—contrary to the Palestinian claim that the Jews uprooted Arabs who had lived in the land uninterrupted for 1,300 years.[42]

"The myth of a stable and settled Palestinian–Arab–Muslim population that had lived in villages and worked the land for centuries, only to be displaced by the Zionist invaders, is simply inconsistent with the recorded demographic data gathered not by the Jews or Zionists but rather by the local authorities themselves," said Dershowitz.[43]

PURCHASED LAND

The Jewish people who immigrated purchased back their homeland from absentee landowners. Wrote Dershowitz, "These landlords were real estate speculators from foreign countries who had no connection to the land and who often exploited the local workers or fellahin."[44]

A study on land purchases in Israel between 1800 and 1948 revealed that three quarters of the land Jewish people purchased during that time was from mega-landowners, rather than from local owners or workers.[45] Even Jordan's King Abdullah admitted "the Arabs are as prodigal in selling their land as they are in … weeping [about it]."[46]

Yet Palestinian propaganda continues to assert the Jews stole the land from local Arabs. Dr. Mitchell Bard, American foreign policy analyst and expert on the Middle East conflict, wrote,

> More than 90 percent of the land Jews had purchased by 1936 had
> been bought from landowners, nearly 40 percent of whom lived in
> Egypt and Syria. Less than 8.7 percent of the Jews' land was purchased
> from the fellaheen. [47]

Dershowitz wrote, "No one who accepts the legitimacy of Australia being an English-speaking Christian nation, or of Western America being part of the United States, can question the legitimacy of the Jewish presence in what is now Israel from the 1880s to the present." While Australia and the United States conquered land through conquest and the use of fear, the Jewish people legally purchased the land that now makes up the modern State of Israel. [48]

JEWISH CLAIM FIVE:
Israel Developed the Barren Land

Mark Twain famously described the barrenness of Palestine after his visit in 1867:

> There is not a solitary village throughout its whole extent. . . . There are
> two or three small clusters of Bedouin tents, but not a single permanent
> habitation. One may ride ten miles hereabouts and not see ten human
> beings. . . . these unpeopled deserts, these rusty mounds of barrenness
> . . . never, never, never do shake the glare from their harsh outlines. [49]

When the Jewish people came to Israel after the First Aliyah, that dismal condition began to change. The Jews came with their hearts and minds set on revitalizing their dear homeland. Although most of the property they purchased consisted of arid desert, the Jewish people used their ingenuity and modern agricultural science to turn a wasteland into a fruit-producing garden.

The April 1960 issue of Scientific American described the barren, unpopulated wasteland the Jewish people encountered when they arrived in the late 20th century:

> *The State of Israel has undertaken to create a new agriculture in an old and damaged land. . . . They came to a land of encroaching sand dunes along a once-verdant coast, of malarial swamps and naked limestone hills. . . . The land of Israel had shared the fate of land throughout the Middle East. A decline in productivity, in population and in culture had set in . . . some 1,300 years ago.[50]*

The writers then proceeded to praise Israel for the feat of transforming such a desolate place into an agricultural, industrious land. They described what a group of 485 farmers from 37 different countries found when they came to Israel to celebrate the nation's 10th anniversary:

> *They found a nation of two million people, whose numbers had doubled in the decade, principally by immigration. . . . [Israel had] nearly achieved the goal of agricultural self-sufficiency. . . . It had more than doubled its cultivated land, to a million acres. It had drained 44,000 acres of marshland and extended irrigation to 325,000 acres; it had increased many-fold the supply of underground water from wells and was far along on the work of diverting and utilizing the scant surface waters. On vast stretches of uncultivable land it had established a new range-cover to support a growing livestock industry and planted 37 million trees in new forests and shelter belts. Israel is . . . seeking full utilization of the land.[51]*

Many Arabs became attracted to Jewish settlements because of such marked improvement in the land, healthcare, education, and job markets. A British official reported in 1937, "The growth in [the numbers of Arab fellahin had been largely due to the health services combating malaria, reducing infant death rates, improving water supply and sanitation."[52] A study on the Jewish settlement of Rishon L'Tzion revealed that a Jewish settlement of 40 Jewish families attracted "more than 400 Arab families." The Arabs families were mostly Bedouins and Egyptians who came to the Jewish settlement and then formed an Arab village in the area.[53]

Israel Obtained International, Legal Recognition

As anti-Semitism began to grow in Europe in the early 1900s, the international community recognized the need for the Jewish people to live in their own national homeland. Great Britain responded to this need through the Balfour Declaration of 1917, and then the United Nations responded in 1947 by voting to partition Palestine into two states: a Jewish state and an Arab state.

BALFOUR DECLARATION

Russian-born Englishman Chaim Weizmann, the leader of the Zionist movement at the time, urged the British to support the creation of an independent Jewish state. In a letter from Lord Balfour to Lord Rothschild, Lord Balfour affirmed the Zionist position and officially recognized the Jewish people's right to a national home in Israel. The letter read,

> *His Majesty's Government view with favour the establishment in Palestine of a national home for the Jewish people, and will use their best endeavours to facilitate the achievement of this object, it being clearly understood that nothing shall be done which may prejudice the civil and religious rights of existing non-Jewish communities in Palestine, or the rights and political status enjoyed by Jews in any other country.*[54]

U.S. President Woodrow Wilson and other Allied leaders endorsed the declaration. The Arabs were outraged.

UN PARTITION PLAN

European anti-Semitism eventually culminated in the Holocaust of World War II. Great Britain closed Palestine's borders so that no Jewish people could immigrate to the land to avoid persecution. Even after the war, the British refused to allow Jewish Holocaust survivors to find refuge in their homeland.[55]

The Jewish people in the land responded to Britain's indifference through an uprising. When the British failed to quell the Jewish revolts, the UN took over. The United Nations Special Committee on Palestine (UNSCOP) began an investigation on the cause of the conflict.[56]

The Jewish community complied, and Menachem Begin—then chief of the Zionist group Irgun—explained his position to UNSCOP: Israel is the land of the Jewish people; there is plenty of room for both Jews and Arabs; and the Jews had to meet force with force against the British.

The Arab community refused to comply with UNSCOP and told the committee the following: Palestine belongs to the Arabs; Jews must be banned from buying land; the European Jewish plight does not concern Palestine; and the Arabs will use force if the UN makes a decision they don't like.[57]

On November 29, 1947, the UN General Assembly officially adopted Resolution 181, which proposed dividing the land into two independent states: an Arab state and a Jewish state. Jerusalem would remain an international zone, belonging to neither state.

Although the plan allotted mostly arid desert to the Jewish state and left its borders indefensible, the Jews accepted the plan anyway. The Arabs, on the other hand, vehemently rejected it and reacted with violence against the Jewish people.[58]

JEWISH CLAIM SEVEN:
Israel Captured Land in Defensive Wars

After the UN Partition Plan, the Arabs rioted and initiated a series of attacks against the Jews. The first large-scale attack fell on January 9,

1948, when approximately 1,000 Arabs attacked Jewish communities. The British surrendered their bases and formed a treaty with Transjordan, which allowed the Arab armies to acquire weapons. The Jews, on the other hand, were prevented from importing any weapons or forming a militia. The British also refused entrance to any Jewish immigrants who sought to help the Jews in Palestine.[59]

The Arabs proudly acknowledged they started a war in response to the partition plan. Jamal Husseini, member of the Arab Higher Committee, told the UN Security Council, "The representative of the Jewish Agency told us yesterday that they were not the attackers, that the Arabs had begun the fighting. We did not deny this. We told the whole world that we were going to fight."[60]

The Jews began to fight back despite their small numbers and shortage of weapons. But while the Arabs aimed to annihilate the Jews, the Jews sought merely to fight for their right to live and remain in their homeland. Mitchell Bard wrote,

> *The Palestinians knew, despite their rhetoric to the contrary, that the Jews were not trying to annihilate them; otherwise, they would not have been allowed to evacuate Tiberias, Haifa, or any of the other towns captured by Jews. . . . The Jews, however, had no place to run had they wanted to. They were willing to fight to the death for their country. It came to that for many because the Arabs were interested in annihilating the Jews.*[61]

THE JEWISH WAR OF INDEPENDENCE

When the British finally left Palestine, Israel officially declared its independence on May 14, 1948, since the United Nations' resolution remained in effect. The Jewish state's Declaration of Independence promoted "liberty, justice, and peace" and promised to "uphold the full social and political equality of all its citizens, without distinction of race, creed, or sex."[62]

The following day, five Arab armies—Egypt, Syria, Transjordan, Lebanon, and Iraq—attacked Israel. The Arab armies had superior terrain, an endless supply of weapons, and 80,000 fighters. Although the Jewish army had far fewer fighters and weapons, it defeated the

Arab armies. Yet not without a severe cost: Israel lost 6,373 Jewish lives and incurred more than $500 million in military expenditures.[63]

Because the Arabs rejected the UN Partition Plan and instead waged war against Israel, they lost some of the land they were originally promised in the plan. Israel had hoped to exchange the gained land for peace, but the Arabs continued to reject the legitimacy of a Jewish state and thus refused to negotiate with Israel after the war.[64] (At this time, Egypt controlled the Gaza Strip; Jordan controlled Judea and Samaria; and Syria controlled the Golan Heights.)

THE SIX-DAY WAR

Some pro-Palestinian advocates argue Israel started the Six-Day War, so Israel should therefore return the land it captured in the war and revert back to its pre-1967 borders.

Two such accusers are Eva Bjoreng, secretary general of Norwegian People's Aid, and Steinar Sorlie, secretary general of Norwegian Refugee Council. They wrote, "In 1967 Israel started the Six Day War by launching an air attack on Egypt, Jordan, Syria and Iraq. Israel occupied East Jerusalem, the West Bank and Gaza and 1.5 million Arabs, mostly Palestinians, came under Israeli occupation."[65] While it is true that Israel fired the first shot against Egypt, the Arab nations of Egypt, Syria, and Jordan actually began the war prior to Israel's pre-emptive attack.

In 1960, Israeli Foreign Minister Golda Meir urged Arab leaders to meet with Israeli Prime Minister David Ben-Gurion for peace talks. But Arab leaders refused. Egyptian President Gamal Abdel Nasser responded by saying Egypt would never recognize the legitimacy of Israel.[66]

The Palestine Liberation Organization (PLO) officially formed in 1964 during the Arab League Summit in Cairo, Egypt. Its members agreed to the Palestine National Charter, which called for the destruction of Israel and the liberation of Palestine.[67] Nasser summed up the Arabs' ambition: "[We desire] the full restoration of the rights of the Palestinian people. In other words, we aim at the destruction of the State of Israel. The immediate aim: perfection of Arab military might. The national aim: the eradication of Israel."[68]

The PLO thus began a series of terror attacks against Israeli civilians: 35 raids in 1965, 41 raids in 1966, and 37 within the first four months of 1967. While Syria and Egypt issued the orders, guerilla fighters from Jordan, the Gaza Strip, and Lebanon carried out the attacks.

From 1965 to 1966, the Syrian army consistently shelled Israeli civilians from the Golan Heights. Children living on kibbutzim were forced to sleep and hide in bomb shelters. When Israel pressured the UN to stop the Syrian aggression, the UN did nothing. So Israel had to defend itself.[69]

On April 7, 1967, Israel retaliated by shooting down six Syrian fighter planes.[70] The UN responded by decrying Israel.[71]

One month later, the tensions increased. On May 15, Egyptian troops moved into Sinai near the Israeli border. Three days later, the Syrian troops gathered along the Golan Heights; and on May 22, Egypt closed the Straits of Tiran to Israeli shipping.[72] The international community recognized Egypt's move as an act of war. Egypt's president himself stated, "We knew the closing of the Gulf of Aqaba meant war with Israel. . . . the objective will be Israel's destruction."[73]

By June 4, 465,000 Arab troops, 2,800 tanks, and 800 aircraft surrounded Israel. Nasser stated,

The armies of Egypt, Jordan, Syria, and Lebanon are poised on the borders of Israel . . . to face the challenge, while standing behind us are the armies of Iraq, Algeria, Kuwait, Sudan, and the whole Arab nation. This act will astound the world. Today they will know that the Arabs are arranged for battle.[74]

Israel's only chance of victory was to launch a surprise, preemptive attack. On June 5, Israel's air force bombed Egyptian airfields while their pilots were eating breakfast. Next, Israel attacked the Jordanian and Syrian air forces. "By the end of the first day," Bard wrote, "nearly the entire Egyptian and Jordanian air forces, and half the Syrians', had been destroyed on the ground."[75]

On June 5, Israeli Prime Minister Levi Eshkol told Jordan's King Hussein that Israel would not attack Jordan unless Jordan first initiated an attack. Dershowitz explained, "Israel made it clear that it had no designs on the West Bank or even on the Jewish Quarter of Jerusalem, with its Western Wall, unless it were to be attacked."[76]

But Hussein ordered the shelling of western Jerusalem. The Jordanians shelled large population centers and residential areas, wounding 1,000 civilians. Israel issued a response attack but quickly accepted a ceasefire at the UN's urging. Jordan continued to fight. "Only then," Dershowitz wrote, "did Israel capture the West Bank and the Old City of Jerusalem—plainly in a defensive war against Jordan started by Jordan after Israel made it clear it wanted no military conflict."[77]

On June 10, Israel accepted a ceasefire encouraged by the United States. Israel's victory resulted in the tripling of its landmass: It unified Jerusalem and captured the Sinai, Golan Heights, Gaza Strip, and Judea and Samaria. But Israel was willing to give up land it had gained in exchange for peace. The PLO, however, still refused to recognize the existence of a Jewish state, and, instead of seeking peace, increased its terrorism against Israel.

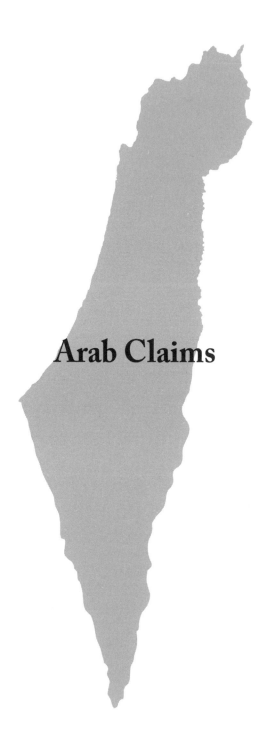

Arab Claims

ARAB CLAIM ONE:

Because Allah Said So!

Like the Jewish people, the Arabs also believe God gave them the Land of Palestine. The Arabs base this claim on two assertions: (1) Arabs are descendants of Abraham through his son Ishmael, and (2) Israel transgressed against God and therefore forfeited its claim to the Promised Land. God's promise to make of Ishmael a "great nation" (Gen. 17:20) now includes the Promised Land (although the Qur'an never mentions "Palestine" or "Jerusalem" as Muslim holy sites).[1] So, who is right?

ARE THE ARABS REALLY DESCENDANTS OF ISHMAEL?

Historical and archaeological evidence says no. The Qur'an claims, "Abraham in truth was not a Jew, neither a Christian; but he was a Muslim . . . and we made a covenant with Abraham and Ishmael" (Sura 3:60; 2:110). But the Bible says Abraham was a Mesopotamian pagan—not a Jew, Muslim, Christian, or Arab.[2]

The proof, both historical and biblical, that Ishmael was the father of the Arab race is sorely lacking. Semitic specialist S. D. Goiten wrote, "There is nothing in the Bible to indicate that Ishmael was the forefather of the Arabs, nor was this belief of the ancient Arabs."[3]

Historically, there is no sure tie between the biblical Ishmael and the modern Arab race. Randall Price explained, "The historical uncertainty arises from the fact that the proper noun Ishmael later became used as a common noun to describe desert tribes in general, such as the Midianites (Judges 8:24; cf. 7:12), whose lineage is traced to a different son of Abraham through his second wife, Keturah (Genesis 25:2)."[4]

HAVE THE ARABS SUPERSEDED THE JEWISH PEOPLE AS GOD'S CHOSEN?

"Certainly not!" in the words of the Jewish apostle Paul. "Has God cast away His people?" Paul asked hypothetically. "Certainly not! For I am an Israelite, of the seed of Abraham, of the tribe of Benjamin. God has not cast away His people whom He foreknew" (Rom. 11:1–2). Paul reaffirmed the Old Testament teaching that God's covenant with Abraham, Isaac, and Jacob was eternal and unconditional.

Muslims claim, however, that we cannot trust the biblical record because the Torah and the Gospels have been corrupted. They claim Paul, specifically, changed the Gospels.[5] This claim is wrong on two accounts. First, the Qur'an itself contradicts that notion. The Qur'an teaches that Allah gave the Law (Torah), the Psalms, and the Gospels:

> *And in their footsteps We sent Jesus the son of Mary, confirming the Law that had come before him: We sent him the Gospel: therein was guidance and light, and confirmation of the Law that had come before him: a guidance and an admonition to those who fear Allah* (Surah 5:46; cf. 2:87; 3:3; 4:163).[6]

The Qur'an also teaches that Allah's words cannot be changed: "There is none that can alter the words of Allah" (Sura 6:34; cf. 6:115; 10:64).[7] So if Allah gave the Torah, the Psalms, and the Gospels—and no one can alter His words—then, according to the Qur'an, we should believe what the Bible says about the land of Israel and the Jewish people.

And, if we believe God revealed Himself through the Bible, we must reject the Qur'an, which came about 600 years after the completed canon of Scripture. The two books are mutually exclusive; both teach radically different ideas about the nature of God, the history of Israel, and who Jesus is.[8]

Furthermore, Muslims have no historical evidence to back up their claim that people have corrupted and changed the words of Scripture. In fact, the New Testament is the best attested to and most reliable work of antiquity. More than 5,600 first-century Greek New Testament manuscripts exist today to verify the fact that our modern Bibles contain the same message the New Testament writers originally recorded:[9] that the God of heaven and Earth chose a specific people—the Jewish people; gave them a specific land—the Land of Israel; and promised them a specific Deliverer—the Messiah, who would save all who believe in Him, "for the Jew first and also for the Greek [Gentile]" (Rom. 1:16).

ARAB CLAIM TWO:

The Arabs Had a Legal Promise

Palestinians claim Sir Henry MacMahon of Great Britain promised the Land of Palestine to the Arabs in the MacMahon-Hussein Correspondence on October 24, 1915. On that day, MacMahon sent a letter to Hussein ibn 'Ali, sherif of Mecca, promising the Arabs land in return for their help in defeating the Ottoman Empire.

However, the letter nowhere mentioned Palestine. Arabs claim the British deliberately omitted the word Palestine from the correspondence so that they could renege on their promise.

But MacMahon claimed he had never offered the land to the Arabs and that Hussein had understood that at the time of the letter. Randall Price said that after the war, the British assumed the Arabs would create a pan-Arab state over the entire eastern Levant and that the Jews would then secure their homeland in Palestine as promised in the Balfour Declaration of 1917.

Thus the British Royal Commission stated in 1937, "If King Hussein and Emir Faisal [Hussein's son] secured their big Arab state . . . they would concede little Palestine to the Jews."[10]

ARAB CLAIM THREE:

The Arabs Had an Ancient and Continuous Presence in the Land

Some claim the Arab Palestinians descended from the ancient Canaanites, Jebusites, and Philistines and thus have lived in the land for more than 5,000 years.

Social anthropologist David Seddon said such a conclusion makes sense since Palestinian is the Greek and Latin term for Philistine. He wrote, "The existence of a population with a recognizably similar name ('the Philistines') in biblical times suggests a degree of continuity over a long historical period (much as 'the Israelites' of the Bible suggest a long historical continuity in the same region)."[11]

Pakistani economist Muhammad Shahid Alam concurs and further asserts that the Arab people's roots are far deeper in the land than those of the Jewish people: "[The Palestinians'] Canaanite roots were more ancient than Isaiah, Ezekiel, David and Moses."[12]

But archaeology and history disagree with such claims in the following ways:

- The Philistines and Jebusites were non-Semitic peoples.
- The Jebusites disappeared from history at the end of the 10th century BC.
- The Philistines disappeared from history in 600 BC when King Nebuchadnezzar of Babylon took them captive.
- History reveals no trace of Canaanite existence in the land up to 1,000 years before any Arab Muslims arrived.
- The Bible distinguishes between "Arabs" and the Philistines (2 Chr. 17:11).
- Neither the Qur'an nor any Muslim writings after the Arab conquest mention Canaanite, Philistine, or Jebusite ancestries.
- Secular history first mentions the Arabs in the Neo-Assyrian annals of the ninth to seventh centuries BC.
- The mere nominal link of Palestinian to Philistine holds no weight since the land did not even receive the name Palestine until AD 135. (The Roman Emperor Hadrian named the land Palestine to punish the Jews for their revolt, because the Philistines were Israel's ancient enemies.)[13]

Some pro-Palestinian sources—instead of arguing the Palestinians descended from the ancient inhabitants of the land—simply argue the land belongs to the Palestinians because of their long residency there since the time of the Muslim conquest. These sources at least grant the fact that Arabs first arrived in Palestine in AD 638, following the Persian and Roman conquests.

Their arrival began a period of Islamic dominance that lasted until 1917. But even during most of this period, the Arabs in Palestine were ruled by foreign Islamic powers. They never had a nation of their own—nor did they desire one, until recently. (See section titled "History of Palestinian Nationalism.") Muslim Turks and Kurds ruled over the region throughout much of that time.[14] Historian David George Hogarth explained:

> *When we look back at the history of the early Caliphate, we find the period of genuine Arab empire extraordinarily short. . . . Arabs governed Arabs, though Arabs on an imperial scale for much less than a century, just the Umayyad Damascus period and no more.*[15]

Nor were Arabs the sole inhabitants of the land. Many other people groups—including the Turks, Greeks, Jews, Armenians, Persians, Georgians, Algerians, and the Sudanese—dwelt in Palestine. Oxford scholar Robert MacAlister, in a 1911 article for Encyclopedia Britannica, described Palestine as a land inhabited by many different "ethnological" groups that spoke "no less than fifty languages."[16]

An 1882 census revealed that fewer than 250,000 Arabs lived in the land. Most were Bedouins (nomads) or fellahin (migrant workers), the majority of whom had either immigrated to work for Zionist settlers or had descended from Arabs who immigrated to the land within the previous 70 years.[17] Historical surveys reveal modern Palestinians are descendants of these workers who came from many nationalities.[18] Price described the atmosphere during that time: "There was no national 'Palestine' nor were there 'Palestinians' who had a distinct identity or private ownership of 'Palestinian' land."[19]

So when did the notions of modern Palestine and the Palestinian people originate?

History of Palestinian Nationalism

PALESTINIANS HAVE SOUGHT TO REWRITE HISTORY.

Contrary to what they are selling the masses, the Palestinians have never existed as a people group or possessed a sovereign nation called "Palestine." And—until the 1960s—the Arabs never even sought an independent state in the land. Instead, Islamic culture historically eschewed nationalism in favor of the greater Islamic community.[1]

During the entire period of Muslim dominance (AD 638–1918), the Muslims never once used the terms Palestine or Palestinian. The word Palestinian, in their minds, was a Jewish term and robbed them of their Arab identity since they had immigrated to the land from Egypt, Syria, and Transjordan.[2] By the early 1920s, their ultimate goal was to unite the land to the rest of the Arab world as a part of Greater Syria: a cultural (not political) unit that encompassed the modern states of Syria, Lebanon, Israel, and Jordan.[3]

Arab leader Auni Bey Abdul-Hadi told the British in 1936, "There is no such country [as Palestine]! Palestine is a term the Zionists invented! . . . Palestine is alien to us; it is the Zionists who introduced it. Our country was for centuries part of Syria."[4]

Arab historian Philip Hitti likewise testified in 1946, "There is no such thing as Palestine in [Arab] history, absolutely not."[5]

That is why no dictionary, encyclopedia, or history book records any mention of the term *Palestinian* in reference to Arabs prior to the creation of the State of Israel in 1948. Until then, the term was used mostly to denote Jewish people living in the land. But after the establishment of Israel, Jewish people assumed the title of Israelis.[6] Randall Price wrote,

In 1947, when UNSCOP was investigating the cause of violence in Palestine and listening to the demands of Arab leaders, there was never any mention of "Palestinians" nor a demand for the establishment of a Palestinian state, nor was this ever made a part of any debate in the United Nations. The plain reason for this is that there was no Palestinian nationalism at this time. Palestinians did not have a separate identity from the Arab culture and accepted the Arab goal in Palestine, which was not political independence in the Land, but an Arab state that would be reunited to the Arab Islamic world.[7]

SO WHEN DID PALESTINIAN NATIONALISM BEGIN?

A form of it began in 1963 with the formation of the PLO. But even then, the PLO's goal was not to form an independent Palestinian state; its goal was to replace Israel with the Arab state of Jordan (instead of Syria).

Jordan's King Hussein stated in 1968, "Jordan is Palestine and Palestine is Jordan."[8]

PLO leader Yasser Arafat likewise stated in 1974, "What you call Jordan is actually Palestine."[9]

The 1967 Six-Day War attests to the fact the Arab-Israeli conflict was not about a struggle for an independent Palestinian state. When the Arab armies surrounded Israel, they were not fighting for "Palestinian" land. At that time, Egypt controlled Gaza; Syria controlled the Golan Heights; and Jordan (illegally) controlled Judea and Samaria. They were fighting to annihilate Israel.

When Israel captured those areas during the war, the Arab nations sought to recapture those lands for themselves, not for a "Palestinian" nation. Price explained,

There were no negotiations with Palestinians after the Arab wars with Israel. For this reason the term "Palestinian(s)" does not appear in any of the foundational documents related to resolving the Arab-Israeli conflicts of the 1967 Six-Day War, the 1973 Yom Kippur War, or UN Security Council Resolutions 242 and 338.[10]

Palestinian nationalism as we know it today began in the mid-1970s, when the PLO realized it would be more politically advantageous to disguise its efforts to destroy Israel in nationalist expressions as a struggle against Israeli "occupation."[11] So after years of denying the existence of a Palestine and a Palestinian people, the Arabs tactfully morphed into an oppressed, indigenous people group called the Palestinians who have lived in the historical nation of Palestine for thousands of years.

The Disputed
Territories

On June 29, 2016, 13-year-old Hallel Yaffa Ariel settled quietly into bed at her home in the Jewish community of Kiryat Arba in Judea and Samaria after a long night of dancing at her recital in front of friends and family. Little did she know that night would be her last dance recital, ever.

The next morning, 17-year-old Arab-Palestinian Muhammad Nasser Tarayrah from the nearby Palestinian village of Bani Na'im snuck through Kiryat Arba's security perimeter, climbed into the house through a window, entered Hallel's bedroom, and brutally stabbed her to death.

Hallel was only in eighth grade and had plans to become a zoologist. Her mother described her as "a flower, a pure soul," and "the light of my life."[1]

What caused Hallel's murderer to commit such a gruesome act of violence against an innocent little girl? Arab Palestinians claim such acts of terrorism are due to Israel's "occupation" of Judea and Samaria. They claim Israel's settlements in the region hinder peace.

Israeli Prime Minister Benjamin Netanyahu commented on the absurdity of such a claim: "You don't murder a sleeping child for peace. You don't slit a girl's throat to protest a policy you don't like. You do this because you've been brainwashed. . . . by a warped ideology that teaches you that this child isn't human."[2]

Many in the international community have hopped on the Palestinian bandwagon, claiming that Israel illegally occupies Judea and Samaria and that its occupation is the main obstacle to peace in the Arab-Israeli conflict.

In a September 2016 speech to the UN General Assembly, Palestinian President Mahmoud Abbas stated, "Israel must . . . put an end to its occupation of our land so the state of Palestine can co-exist alongside the state of Israel in peace and security as good neighbours."[3]

The Palestinian argument is untrue based on two facts: (1) Israel has the legal right to reside in the West Bank, and (2) The Arab-Palestinians' refusal to recognize Israel's right to exist is the true barrier to peace—not Jewish settlements.

ISRAEL'S LEGAL "OCCUPATION"

Israel gained control of the "occupied" territories—Gaza and the West Bank—after its victory in the Six-Day War, a defensive war Israel launched against the Arab countries that had surrounded Israel in an attempt to destroy the Jewish state. Countries legally have the right to acquire territory in wars of self-defense and afterward to require conditions of peace and security before withdrawal. In fact, the UN had never before ordered a nation to return any territory captured in a defensive war until Israel's capture of the West Bank.[4]

The term *occupation* does not even legally apply to the West Bank because no nation sovereignly controlled the area. It did not belong to "Palestine," but Transjordan had been illegally occupying it since 1948. So "disputed territories" more accurately describes the region.[5]

Palestinians claim Israel's occupation of the West Bank violates UN Resolution 242. But that is not true. The resolution calls for the "withdrawal of Israeli armed forces from territories occupied in the recent conflict," but it also calls for "termination of all claims or states of belligerency" and recognition that "every State in the area" has the "right to live in peace within secure and recognized boundaries, free from threats or acts of force."[6]

The resolution's call for Israel's withdrawal is contingent upon the Arabs' acceptance of Israel's legitimacy as a state and their willingness to live in peace. The Arabs, realizing the resolution called for accepting Israel's existence and making peace with the Jewish state, vehemently opposed the resolution.

Instead, they met at a summit in Khartoum and issued the famous "three no's" statement: "No peace with Israel, no negotiations with Israel, no recognition of Israel." They also wrote and adopted the Palestinian National Charter that expressly denied Israel's right to exist and promised to fight until it liberated all of Palestine.[7]

Israel, however, accepted the resolution. In a May 1, 1968, statement to the UN Security Council, Israeli Ambassador Abba Eban declared,

My government has indicated its acceptance of the Security Council resolution for the promotion of agreement on the establishment of a just and lasting peace. I am also authorized to reaffirm that we are willing to seek agreement with each Arab State on all matters included in that resolution.[8]

It is also important to note that the resolution does not call for Israel to withdraw from all territories. British Ambassador Lord Caradon deliberately omitted the word *all*, recognizing Israel's need for more defensible borders. He explained, "It would have been wrong to demand that Israel return to its positions of June 4, 1967, because those positions were undesirable and artificial."[9] Prior to the Six-Day War, Israel's borders were practically indefensible and placed the nation in constant danger because of its surrounding hostile enemies.

THE TRUE BARRIER TO PEACE

As already stated, Palestinians claim Israeli settlements are the major barrier to peace. But if this were true, why was peace absent prior to 1967—before Israel "occupied" any so-called Palestinian territories? The answer: The true barrier to peace has never been Israel's settlements in Judea and Samaria but, rather, the Arab-Palestinians' refusal to accept Israel's existence.

Before 1967, when Jordan controlled Judea and Samaria (1948–1967), Arabs refused to let any Jews live there and refused to make peace with Israel.[10] Also prior to 1967 (and therefore prior to the issue of the settlements), the Arabs formed the PLO whose main stated goal was to destroy Israel. The PLO carried out a host of terrorist activities against Israel—long before Israel gained control of Gaza, Judea, and Samaria.

Israel has consistently displayed its desire for peace, even to the point of giving up land crucial to its safety. The Arab Palestinians, on the other hand, have consistently demonstrated their true goal: to annihilate Israel and replace the Jewish state with an Arab state—free from Jews.

After the Six-Day War, Israel offered to exchange most of its conquered land for peace. Israel immediately accepted UN Resolution 242, while the Arabs uniformly rejected it. Israeli historian Benny Morris wrote, "The Israeli government hoped to convert its stunning military victory into a political achievement: the conquered territories could be traded for peace."[11]

On June 19, 1967, Israel offered to give up the Sinai and Golan to Egypt and Syria in exchange for peace. The Arab states rejected the offer, still refusing to admit defeat against its desire to wipe out Israel.[12]

In 1977, Egypt finally came to a peace agreement with Israeli Prime Minister Menachem Begin. Israel demonstrated its willingness to give up land in keeping with UN Resolution 242 since Egypt agreed to recognize Israel and seek peace. Israel dismantled its settlements in the Sinai and turned the area over to Egypt. Begin also halted settlement building in hopes that other Arab states would join Egypt in seeking peace with Israel. None did.[13]

In 2000, former Israeli Prime Minister Ehud Barak offered an enormous land concession to then president of the Palestinian National Authority, Yasser Arafat. He offered Arafat 97 percent of the West Bank, full control of Gaza, the right of return for Palestinian refugees, $30 billion for reparations, the Arab neighborhoods in eastern Jerusalem and control of their holy places, and extra land near Gaza to make up for the 3 percent of land in the West Bank that would remain in Israel's control. Barak said Arafat must only concede to allow Jewish control of the Western Wall, the part of the Temple Mount dear to the Jewish people.

Arafat rejected Barak's outlandishly generous offer. He did not want Israel to control any part of the Temple Mount; he rejected the security arrangements because he did not want Jewish planes flying over Palestinian land; and he did not want to agree to end the conflict. Instead, Arafat again resorted to terrorism and violence against Israel.

Daniel Kurtzer, former U.S. ambassador to Israel and Egypt, said of the peace negotiations, "The failure of Camp David is largely attributed to the fact that Arafat did not even negotiate. . . . He put nothing on the table."[14]

In 2005, Israel again made a huge concession for peace: unilateral withdrawal from the Gaza Strip. Israel uprooted 9,500 Jewish people from their homes—men, women, and children who had lived in their privately owned homes for decades and built their businesses and lives in the region.[15] Israel gave the Palestinians a Jew-free Gaza Strip.

How did Arab-Palestinians respond? By using the disengagement as an opportunity to fire more rockets from Gaza into Israel. In the year following Israel's withdrawal, Gaza fired 1,123 rockets into the Jewish state. And from the time of disengagement through 2018, ter-rorists launched more than 11,000 rockets into Israel, many of which targeted Israeli towns.[16]

In 2007, Hamas became the governing authority in Gaza. Its charter explicitly calls for the destruction of Israel by jihad (war) and the murder of the Jewish people. It views the Arab-Israeli conflict as a religious war of Islam against the infidels (Jews and Christians). Several lines of the charter read, "Israel will exist, and will continue to exist, until Islam abolishes it." "The Prophet, Allah's prayer and peace be upon him, says: 'The hour of judgment shall not come until the Muslims fight the Jews and kill them.'"[17]

In 2008, Israel's Prime Minister Ehud Olmert made Palestinian Authority President Mahmoud Abbas an unprecedented offer. He offered to place Jerusalem's Old City under international control and withdraw from all Arab neighborhoods in eastern Jerusalem. He also told Abbas Israel would almost completely disengage from Judea and Samaria, remaining in only 6.3 percent of the territory in order to maintain major Jewish settlements. And—he added—Israel would compensate for the remaining land in Judea and Samaria by offering the Arabs 5.8 percent of Israel's land. Security checks would also be removed between Gaza and Judea and Samaria to provide for a contiguous Palestinian state.[18]

Abbas rejected the offer, again demonstrating the truth that the lack of peace in the Arab-Israeli conflict is not due to Israel's failure to make concessions for peace. It is due to the Arabs' failure to make concessions for peace or accept the fact of Israel's statehood. Abbas's spokesman said of Olmert's proposal,

> *The Israeli proposal is not acceptable. The Palestinian side will only accept a Palestinian state with territorial continuity, with holy Jerusalem as its capital, without settlements, and on the June 4, 1967 boundaries.*[19]

Israel has consistently demonstrated its desire for peace with its Arab neighbors. It has repeatedly shown its willingness to make land concessions in exchange for peace. But the Arabs, time after time, have displayed their refusal to make peace with Israel because of their underlying hatred for the Jewish people and unwillingness to accept Israel's right to exist.

ISRAEL'S RIGHTS TO THE "DISPUTED TERRITORIES"

Overall, Israel has withdrawn from 94 percent of the territories it won in the 1967 war: all of Sinai, all of the Gaza Strip, more than 40 percent of Judea and Samaria, and part of the Golan Heights.[20] Israel made these concessions even though it maintains the legal, historical, biblical, and moral rights to live in those territories: Legal, because it won the territories in a war of self-defense and because Jewish people legally bought and owned private land in those areas. Historical, because the Jewish people have ancient ties to the land and have maintained a continuous presence in it. Biblical, because God gave the Jewish people those territories as part of the Promised Land. And moral, because Jewish people have just as much right to live in those areas as they would in your hometown.

Commenting on the Arab claim that the absence of peace is due to the Jewish presence in Judea and Samaria, Netanyahu said in a September 2016 Facebook video post, "The Palestinian leadership . . . demands a Palestinian state with one precondition: No Jews. There's a phrase for that. It's called 'ethnic cleansing.' And this demand is outrageous."[21]

While Israel allows Arab-Palestinians to live in the Jewish state peacefully and with full citizenship rights, the Arabs demand a land free from all Jews. Such a demand screams anti-Semitism and discrimination.

The Jewish people have lived in the West Bank since ancient times. Mitchell Bard, commenting on the ancient and continuous Jewish presence in Judea and Samaria, wrote,

> *Some settlements, such as in Hebron, existed throughout the centuries of Ottoman rule, while others were established prior to the establishment of the State of Israel. Many present-day Israeli settlements were established on sites that were homes to Jewish communities in previous generations, long before 1948.*[22]

Furthermore, the settlements that were built on the ancient Jewish homeland after 1967 were built with the supervision of Israel's Supreme Court to ensure that no communities were established on private Arab land and that no Arabs were displaced.[23]

Jewish settlements cover merely 1.5 percent of the land in Judea and Samaria.[24] A December 31, 2015, report from Israel's Interior Ministry showed 406,302 Jewish people dwell in these communities.[25] Two-thirds of the region's total Jewish inhabitants live in only five blocs: Ma'ale Adumim, Modi'in Illit, Ariel, Gush Etzion, and Givat Ze'ev. These blocs equate to five major American cities.[26] The Arab demand for the expulsion of all Jews from the region is unreasonable, immoral, and racist.

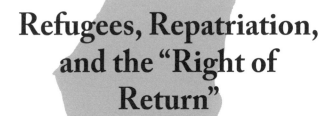

Refugees, Repatriation, and the "Right of Return"

Palestinian rhetoric concerning refugees and the "right of return" storms our media. It paints Israel as a nation of thieves who confiscated the property of 700,000 Arabs who fled their homes in the wake of the War of Independence (1948) and scorns Israel for refusing to allow the refugees and their descendants to return.

Abbas claims, "The right of return is a personal decision.... Neither the PA, nor the state, . . . nor any Palestinian or Arab leader has the right to deprive someone from his right to return."[1]

Ohio State University law professor John Quigley concurs: "A total repatriation, even with a generous financial compensation added for the years of exile, would not fully compensate the Palestinians for what was done to them in 1948."[2]

Such accusations may seem founded until one hears the facts the liberal media and contemporary Palestinian advocates fail to articulate. As Israel's ancient King Solomon wisely wrote, "The first one to plead his cause seems right, until his neighbor comes and examines him" (Prov. 18:17).

POPULATION EXCHANGE

Although attention abounds concerning the 700,000 Arab-Palestinians who fled Israel and became refugees, few outlets talk about the 860,000 Jewish refugees who were forced to leave their homes in Israel's surrounding Arab countries because of increased persecution surrounding the 1948 war.[3]

Why do the media and United Nations pay no attention to the Jewish refugee crisis? Because it no longer exists. Israel settled the refugees in temporary transit camps until they could be fully integrated into developed towns and neighborhoods. The last Jewish refugee camp in Israel closed around 1963.[4]

While Israel sought to remedy the Jewish refugee problem, the Arab states refused to integrate the Palestinian refugees and instead sought to use them as a key political tool to perpetuate the Arab-Israeli conflict and demonize Israel. Jordan is the only state that granted any refugees citizenship.[5]

Summarizing the Arab-Jewish population exchange, Randall Price explained, "No doubt, historic injustices have occurred with respect to refugees, but they have occurred for both peoples sharing the same Land.

Therefore, the claim of one people to the Land on this basis cannot be made in exclusion of the other."[6]

ASSETS EXCHANGE

Not only did a population exchange take place between the Jewish and Arab states, but an exchange of assets took place as well.

Palestinians frequently cite UN General Assembly Resolution 194 to argue for reparations and the right of return. The resolution (summarized) states,

- The refugees' countries of origin should allow the refugees (Jewish and Arab) to return if they will live at peace with their neighbors.
- Those countries should provide reparations for assets of refugees who choose not to return.
- Resettlement in other countries is a reasonable option.[7]

When the UN introduced the resolution in 1948, all the Arab states vehemently opposed it and voted against it. They refused to assent to the resolution's implicit recognition of Israel as a sovereign state. But in the 1960s, they decided to reclaim the resolution and argue for their "right of return."[8]

Such an Arab claim is hypocritical to say the least, considering the fact that Jewish people could not return to their countries of origin nor receive compensation for their lost assets. For example, Jews who fled Judea and Samaria during the wake of the 1948 war left behind all of their assets, and Jordan—which assumed control of the area—refused to compensate them or even allow any Jews in the region for the 19 years in which it ruled.[9]

Such was the fate of the hundreds of thousands of Jewish refugees who fled their homes in Arab countries around 1948 (as well as the hundreds of thousands of Jewish people who were forced out of Arab states during World War II). Such countries as Iraq, Egypt, and Syria began to severely persecute their Jewish communities because of their anger toward the establishment of a Jewish state. Jews were branded as Zionist enemies of the state; and they were looted, arrested, and killed. Some fled of their own volition because of the violent persecution, and some were forcefully expelled.[10]

The Arab states assumed all of the assets of their Jewish citizens, many of whom had been living in those lands for generations, even prior to the Muslim conquest.[11] In Iraq alone, the government seized $243 million ($6 billion in today's terms) of Jewish assets.[12] Iraq's Prime Minister Nuri Said claimed the money would serve as retribution for the confiscation of Palestinian assets in Israel.

At the Paris conference in 1951, Israel demanded a link be created between Jewish assets and Palestinian assets, but the request was ignored. As a result, Israel had no other option but to pass its own law, which allowed the government to use Arab-Palestinian assets left behind to aid the influx of Jewish refugees from Arab countries.

Comparing the value of Jewish assets absorbed by the Arab states with the value of Palestinian assets absorbed by the Jewish state reveals a massive disparity: Palestinian assets totaled $3.4 billion and Jewish assets totaled a whopping $100 billion.[13] But Palestinian advocates conveniently ignore such facts and focus solely on Israel's need to repatriate the Palestinians.

Dr. Shaul Bartal, lecturer in Middle Eastern Studies at Bar Ilan University, explained:

> *According to U.N. data, the total value of Palestinian assets is lower than just the minimum estimate of the confiscated assets of Iraq's Jews. . . . In other words, any Palestinian demand for reparations has been paid many times over although the funds went to their host Arab countries.*[14]

PROBLEM PERPETUATED

While Israel settled the Jewish refugees, the Arabs and the United Nations Relief and Works Agency (UNRWA) have sought to perpetuate the Palestinian refugee problem.

For the first time in its history, the UN created a special refugee agency solely dedicated to aiding the refugees of a specific region: It established UNRWA to help Arab-Palestinians who fled Israel during the 1948 War of Independence. All other refugee issues throughout history and throughout the world have been settled by the UN High Commissioner for Refugees (UNHCR).[15]

The UNHCR defines refugees as those who live outside of their home countries until they either return or resettle in host countries. In stark contrast, UNRWA defines Palestinian refugees as those who lived in Israel prior to 1948 and "the descendants of Palestine refugee males, including legally adopted children" and states that they will maintain their status as refugees until they return.[16]

Because of UNRWA's definition, much of its registered "refugees" are actually people who resettled and became citizens of Jordan.[17] If one applies the UNHCR definition—the standard the UN applies to refugees in all other regions of the world—only about 50,000 Palestinian refugees exist today. Yet UNRWA and Palestinian spokespeople claim there are more than 5 million Palestinian refugees today (a number that grew from the 700,000 actual refugees in 1948).[18]

James Lindsay, a former legal advisor for UNRWA from 2000 to 2007, presented a monograph to the Washington Institute for Near East Policy in 2009 in which he concluded, "The vast majority of UNRWA's registered refugees have already been 'resettled' (or, to use the UN euphemism, 'reintegrated')." He said the "only thing preventing citizens from ceasing to be 'refugees' is UNRWA's singular definition of what constitutes a refugee." He then recommended UNRWA hand over the refugee issue to Jordan.[19]

Problem Solved. Quigley called the Palestinian refugee problem "the most critical issue standing in the way of an Israeli-Palestinian peace."[20] But Israel has already fulfilled its reparations obligation according to UN Resolution 194 because the Arab states absorbed more than $100 billion in Jewish refugee assets. The Arabs hold Israel to a standard they refuse to adhere to themselves regarding the hundreds of thousands of Jewish refugees.

Even former UNRWA spokesman Andrew Whitley admitted in a 2010 speech, "We recognize, as I think most do, although it's not a position that we publicly articulate, that the right of return is unlikely to be exercised to the territory of Israel to any significant or meaningful extent. . . . It's not a politically palatable issue." UNRWA promptly condemned him after his speech, and Whitley recanted.[21]

Israel seeks peace with its Arab neighbors, but it cannot sacrifice its safety or statehood by granting 700,000 refugees and their 4 million descendants a "right of return." If Israel allowed all UNRWA-registered refugees to return to Israel, it would no longer be a Jewish state; it would be quickly consumed by a people utterly bent on its destruction. (Hamas appoints UNRWA staff and promotes the anti-Semitic, anti-Israel rhetoric in UNRWA schools.[22])

Overall peace and a solution to the Palestinian refugee issue will only take place when UNRWA and Palestinian advocates (1) admit that most registered refugees are not actual refugees, (2) seek to resettle actual refugees in their host Arab countries, and (3) accept the legitimacy of the Jewish state. The Arabs, therefore, are responsible for creating the refugee issue and for perpetuating it. If the Arabs had accepted the UN Partition Plan instead of making war against Israel in 1948, no Arab-Palestinian or Jewish person ever would have become a refugee.

CONCLUSION

The land of Israel belongs to the Jewish people—biblically, historically, and legally:

Biblically, God promised it to them as an eternal possession in a unilateral, unconditional covenant. The supersessionist argument that Israel no longer can claim this promise because the church has replaced Israel crumbles under the scrutiny of Scripture.

Historically, archaeological evidence confirms Israel's ancient presence in the land, contradicting the assertions of Palestinian propaganda. Historical records also confirm the Jewish people have maintained an uninterrupted, continuous presence in the land throughout the centuries.

Legally, the Jewish people bought the majority of land in Israel from absentee landlords, contrary to the Palestinian claim that Israel stole land from indigenous Palestinian inhabitants.

The Balfour Declaration and the UN Partition Plan legally promised the Jewish people a homeland in Palestine. Israel accepted the UN Partition Plan and declared its statehood, a move the international community (except for the Arab states) accepted as legitimate.

The Arabs states rejected the UN Partition Plan (they rejected the plan's offer of an Arab state in the region), refused to accept the notion of a Jewish homeland in Palestine, and began a series of terrorist attacks against Israel.

The Arabs started both the War of Independence in 1948 and the Six-Day War in 1967. Prior to the Arab attacks in 1948, there were no Arab refugees in Israel. Prior to the Arab attacks in 1967, there were no "occupied territories." Such facts reveal the conflict has never been about Israel's "occupation" or refusal to repatriate the refugees, contrary to contemporary Palestinian claims. The conflict has always been about the Arabs' refusal to accept the legitimacy of Israel.

When Israel pushed back the Arab armies and gained "the disputed territories" in the Six-Day War, it did so legally because it won those territories in self-defense. But even though Israel legally acquired Gaza, Judea and Samaria, and Jerusalem, the nation sought to make concessions with the Arabs in hopes of securing peace. The Arabs refused.

The Arab claims of a divine, historical, and legal right to the land fail under investigation:

Biblically, God promised the land to Abraham's son Isaac, not Ishmael—of whom the Arabs claim they are descendants. The Arabs claim Israel forfeited its promises because of disobedience, so the promise went to Ishmael instead. But no historical evidence supports the Muslim claim that they descended from Ishmael, and no historical evidence supports their claim that the Hebrew and Christian Scriptures—which teach God gave the land to Abraham, Isaac, and Jacob—have been corrupted.

Historically, a "Palestinian people" and a country of "Palestine" never existed. No historical source sustains the Palestinians' claim that they descended from the ancient Philistines, Jebusites, or Canaanites. Those people groups disappeared long before any Arab Muslims arrived in the land.

Today's "Palestinians" are descendants of workers who immigrated to the region in modern times from many different surrounding nations.

Until the 1960s, the Arabs eschewed the terms *Palestinian* and *Palestine.* Only with the formation of the PLO did the Arabs in Israel begin a nationalistic rhetoric claiming to be a Palestinian people robbed of their homeland.

Legally, no proof exists for the Arab claim that the MacMahon-Hussein Correspondence promised all of Palestine to the Arabs. On the contrary, records reveal MacMahon claimed he never made such a promise.

We have seen how neither the issue of the "disputed territories" nor Israel's refusal to grant the Palestinians a "right of return" presents obstacles to peace in the Arab-Israeli conflict, contrary to Palestinian claims. Israel has made concession after concession throughout the years in efforts to seek peace with the Palestinians. Each time, Arab leaders have refused Israel's generous propositions and have increased their acts of terrorism.

Israel clearly demonstrated its desire for peace with its unilateral withdrawal from Gaza, a move that came at great cost to the Jewish people. The Palestinians responded by using the region as a base to fire more rockets into Israel.

The true history of the Arab-Israeli conflict reveals Israel is biblically, morally, historically, and legally entitled to the land. It reveals the true intent of the Arab-Palestinians: to extinguish Israel, the only democracy in the Middle East.

ENDNOTES

JEWISH CLAIMS

[1] Randall Price, *Fast Facts on the Middle East Conflict* (Eugene, OR: Harvest House, 2003), 47.

[2] Michael J. Vlach, "Various Forms of Replacement Theology," *The Master's Seminary Journal* (hereafter cited as *TMSJ*) 20, no. 1 (2009): 59 <tms.edu/m/tmsj20d.pdf>.

[3] Ibid., 60.

[4] Ibid., 61.

[5] Ibid.

[6] Ibid., 59.

[7] Vlach, "What Does Christ As 'True Israel' Mean for the Nation Israel?: A Critique of the Non-Dispensational Understanding," *TMSJ* 23, no. 1 (2012): 43 <tms.edu/m/msj23c.pdf>.

[8] Ibid., 47.

[9] Ibid., 45.

[10] Ibid., 44.

[11] Ibid., 47–48.

[12] Ibid., 45–46.

[13] Ibid., 49.

[14] Ibid., 48.

[15] Ibid., 48–49.

[16] Renald E. Showers, *Five Facts You Should Know About Israel* (Bellmawr, NJ: The Friends of Israel Gospel Ministry, ND), 16.

[17] Vlach, "What Does Christ As 'True Israel' Mean for the Nation Israel?" 46–47.

[18] Ibid., 49.

[19] Ibid., 51.

[20] Ibid.

[21] Ibid.

[22] Ibid.

[23] Ibid., 52.

[24] Ibid.

[25] Ibid., 53.

[26] Itamar Marcus and Nan Jacques Zilberdik, "The PA denies Jewish history in Jerusalem: The Jewish Temple is 'the alleged Temple,'" Palestinian Media Watch, August 11, 2011 <palwatch.org/main. aspx?fi=157&doc_id=5452>.

[27] PA TV (Fatah), August 20, 2010, as quoted in Archaeology Verifies the Bible as God's Word, ii. <bibletoday.com/ebook/Archaeology.pdf>.

[28] PA TV (Fatah), January 5, 2012, Ibid., iii.

[29] Ibid., 17–18.

[30] Drew Zahn, "Walk Among the Ruins of Solomon's 1st Temple," WND.com, June 24, 2011 <wnd.com/2011/06/315145/>.

[31] Mitchel Bard, Ph.D., *The Complete Idiot's Guide to Middle East Conflict*, 2nd ed., (Indianapolis, IN, Alpha, 2003), 19.

[32] Price, 47–48.

[33] Ibid.

[34] Mitchell Bard, "Pre-State Israel: Jewish Claim To The Land Of Israel," jewishvirtuallibrary.org <tinyurl.com/y2nl845a>.

[35] Bard, *The Complete Idiot's Guide to Middle East Conflict*, 64.

[36] Ibid.

[37] Rachel Avraham, "Jewish Poets Yearning for Jerusalem throughout History," UnitedWithIsrael.org, May 7, 2013 <tinyurl.com/y4vffzmw>.

[38] Alan Dershowitz, *The Case for Israel* (Hoboken, NJ: John Wiley & Sons, 2003), 22.

[39] Ibid., 24.

[40] Benny Morris, *Righteous Victims* (New York, NY: Vintage Books, 2001), 123, cited in Dershowitz, 25.

[41] Dershowitz, 25.

[42] Jamal Husseini, February 9, 1939, cited in Arieh Avneri, *The Claim of Dispossession* (New Brunswick: Transaction Books, 1984), 11; cited in Dershowitz, 26–28.

[43] Dershowitz, 27.

[44] Ibid., 25.

[45] Ibid.

[46] King Abdullah of Jordan, *My Memoirs Completed*, trans. Harold W. Glidden (London: Longman, 1978), 88–89, cited in Dershowitz, 28.

[47] Bard, *The Complete Idiot's Guide to Middle East Conflict*, 101.

[48] Dershowitz, 6.

[49] Dershowitz, 23.

[50] "50 Years Ago: The Reclamation of a Man-Made Desert," Scientific American <scientificamerican.com/article/reclamation-of-man-made-desert>.

[51] Ibid.

[52] Joan Peters, *From Time Immemorial* (Chicago: JKAP, 1984), 223–224, cited in Dershowitz, 28.

[53] Dershowitz, 27.

[54] Bard, *The Complete Idiot's Guide to Middle East Conflict*, 70.

[55] Ibid., 124.

[56] Ibid., 127–128.

[57] Ibid., 128–130.

[58] Ibid., 133, 136–137.

[59] Ibid., 140–141.

[60] Ibid., 142.

[61] Ibid., 144.

[62] Ibid.

[63] Ibid., 145–149.

[64] Price, 49.

[65] Dershowitz, 91.

[66] "The Six-Day War: Background & Overview," Jewish Virtual Library <jewishvirtuallibrary.org/jsource/History/67_War.html>.

[67] "Palestine Liberation Organization (PLO): History & Overview," Jewish Virtual Library <jewishvirtuallibrary.org/jsource/Terrorism/plo.html>.

[68] Bard, *The Complete Idiot's Guide to Middle East Conflict*, 195.

[69] "The Six-Day War: Background & Overview."

[70] Ibid.

[71] Bard, *The Complete Idiot's Guide to Middle East Conflict*, 195.

[72] Ibid., 196.

[73] Michael Oren, *Six Days of War* (Oxford: Oxford University Press, 2002), 93, cited in Dershowitz, 91–92.

[74] Bard, *The Complete Idiot's Guide to Middle East Conflict*, 197.

[75] Ibid., 198.

[76] Dershowitz, 92–93.

[77] Ibid., 93.

ARAB CLAIMS

1   Price, 50–51.
2   Ibid.
3   S. D. Goiten, *Jews and Arabs: Their Contacts Through the Ages* (New York, NY: Schocken Books, 1964), 121–122, cited in Price, 51.
4   Price, 51.
5   David Wood, "Who Corrupted the Gospel?" answeringmuslims.com, May 25, 2011 <tinyurl.com/4x3yoh5>.
6   Matt Slick, "The Qu'ran says the Bible is not corrupt," CARM: Christian Apologetics & Research Ministry <carm.org/quran-says-bible-not-corrupt>.
7   Ibid.
8   Jonathan McLatchie, "A Simple Reason Why The Qur'an Cannot Be The Word of God," answeringmuslims.com, November 25, 2015 <tinyurl.com/yyzlojly>.
9   Matt Slick, "Manuscript evidence for superior New Testament reliability," CARM: Christian Apologetics & Research Ministry, December 10, 2008 <carm.org/manuscript-evidence>.
10 Price, 53–54.
11 David Seddon, ed. *A Political and Economic Dictionary of the Middle East* (New York, NY: Taylor & Francis, 2004), 532.
12 M. Shahid Alam, "A Colonizing Project Built on Lies," counterpunch .org, April 18, 2002 <tinyurl.com/y4b5bn6d>.
13 Price, 58, 61.
14 Ibid., 52–53.
15 Cited in Eliyahu Tal, *Whose Jerusalem?* (Tel Aviv: International Forum for a United Jerusalem, 1994), 100–101, cited in Price, 53.
16 Dershowitz, 26.
17 Price, 23.
18 Ibid., 62.
19 Ibid., 23.

HISTORY OF PALESTINIAN NATIONALISM

1   Ibid., 22–23.
2   Ibid., 58.
3   Daniel Pipes, "The Year the Arabs Discovered Palestine," Middle East Forum, Summer 1989 <danielpipes.org/8025/the-year-the-arabs-

discovered-palestine>.

4 Cited in *The Jerusalem Post* (November 2, 1991) and by Clarence Wagner, "40 Significant Facts About Israel's History" (Jerusalem: October 2000), 3:3, cited in Price, 25.

5 Ibid., 58.

6 Ibid., 58–59.

7 Cited in Avner Yaniv, *PLO* (Jerusalem: Israel Universities Study Group of Middle Eastern Affairs, August 1974), 5, cited in Price, 59.

8 Ibid., 60.

9 Ibid.

10 Ibid., 59–60.

11 Ibid., 60.

THE DISPUTED TERRITORIES

1 Judah Ari Gross, "Hallel Ariel, 'princess in white,' mourned in Hebron funeral," timesofisrael.com, July 1, 2016 <tinyurl.com/y6t35tdk>.

2 "Netanyahu: 'You don't murder a sleeping child for peace,'" timesofisrael.com, July 1, 2016 <tinyurl.com/y5bqnuoz>.

3 "Abbas to UN: Declare 2017 year to end Israel occupation," AlJazeera .com, September 22, 2016 <tinyurl.com/y4khsqes>.

4 Dershowitz, 96.

5 Mitchell Bard, *On One Foot,* (Chevy Chase, MD: AICE, 2008), 35.

6 Bard, *The Complete Idiot's Guide to Middle East Conflict,* 203.

7 Dershowitz, 97.

8 Bard, *The Complete Idiot's Guide to Middle East Conflict,* 205.

9 Ibid., 203–204.

10 Bard, *On One Foot,* 34.

11 Morris, *Righteous Victims,* 330, cited in Dershowitz, 96.

12 Dershowitz, 97.

13 Bard, *On One Foot,* 34.

14 David Shyovitz, "2000 Camp David Summit: Background & Overview," Jewish Virtual Library <jewishvirtuallibrary.org/jsource/ Peace/cd2000art.html>.

15 Bard, *On One Foot,* 36.

16 "Rocket Attacks on Israel From Gaza," IDF Blog: The Official Blog of the Israel Defense Forces, <idfblog.com/facts-figures/rocket-attacks-toward-israel/>.

[17] "Hamas Charter," CAMERA: Committee for Accuracy in Middle East Reporting in America, January 5, 2009 <camera.org/article/hamas-charter>.

[18] Josef Federman, "Abbas admits he rejected 2008 peace offer from Olmert," timesofisrael.com, November 19, 2015 <tinyurl.com/y2x4n4fp>.

[19] Aluf Benn and Reuters, "PA Rejects Olmert's Offer to Withdraw From 93% of West Bank," Haaretz, August 12, 2008 <haaretz.com/1.5014018>.

[20] Bard, *On One Foot*, 32.

[21] Caroline Glick, "Benjamin Netanyahu and the 'otherwise enlightened,'" Jpost.com, September 12, 2016 <tinyurl.com/y5f579kc>.

[22] Bard, *On One Foot*, 32.

[23] Ibid.

[24] Ibid., 36.

[25] Baruch Gordon, "The precise number of Jews in the 'West Bank,'" Israelnationalnews.com, March 6, 2016 <israelnationalnews.com/News/News.aspx/213234>.

[26] Bard, *On One Foot*, 36.

REFUGEES, REPATRIATION, AND THE "RIGHT OF RETURN"

[1] Alexander Joffe and Asaf Romirowsky, "Return or Die?" The American Interest, May 17, 2015 <the-american-interest.com/2015/05/17/return-or-die/>.

[2] John Quigley, "Palestine Refugee Repatriation in the American Discourse," The New Centennial Review 5, no. 2 (Fall 2008): 284 <https://muse.jhu.edu/article/255116>.

[3] Shabtai Shavit, "A Tale of Two 'Refugee' Organizations: UNRWA vs. UNHCR," JUSTICE 55 (Winter 2014–2015): 37 <tinyurl.com/yy8hadea>.

[4] Shaul Bartal, "The Palestinian Refugee Problem Resolved," The Middle East Quarterly 20, no. 4 (Fall 2013): 39 <meforum.org/meq/pdfs/3643.pdf>.

[5] Alexander Joffe and Asaf Romirowsky, "The Politics Of The Palestinian Right Of Return," Forbes.com, February 24, 2014 <tinyurl.com/y5ogkkso>.

[6] Price, 55.

[7] Bartal, 30.

[8] Ibid.

[9] Price, 54–55.

[10] Bartal, 32–38.

[11] Ibid., 30–31.

[12] Jacob Tovy, *Al Miftan Beita, Hitgabshut Mediniyuta shel Israel Be-Sugiyat Ha-Plitim Ha-Palestinim 1948–1956* (Jerusalem: Herzl Institute for the Study of Zionism and History and Ben Gurion Research Institute 2008), 210, cited in Bartal, 34.

[13] Martin Gilbert, *In Ishmael's House, A History of Jews in Muslim Lands* (Cornwall: Yale University Press, 2010), 329, cited in Bartal, 39.

[14] Bartal, 39.

[15] Shavit, 35.

[16] Ibid., 34.

[17] Bartal, 32.

[18] Shavit, 35.

[19] Asaf Romirowsky, "UNRWA: The Crux of the Arab-Israeli Conflict," JUSTICE 55 (Winter 2014–2015): 12–13 <tinyurl.com/yy8hadea>.

[20] Quigley, 273.

[21] Joffe and Romirowsky, "Return or Die?"

[22] Shavit, 26, 35–39.